The Indescribable Thrill of The Half-Volley

Tim Allen

Leafe Press

Published by Leafe Press
Nottingham, England.
www.leafepresspoetry.com

Copyright © Tim Allen, 2023. All rights reserved.
Cover artwork © Terry Hackman, 2023. All rights reserved.

ISBN: 978-1-7397213-6-7

Cover image: "**Drawing 14**" by Terry Hackman.
Used with kind permission of the artist

1. invisible signature

The photo of nothing in particular was a dry wave
Hidden in its trough - something eating between breaths

The seafront waited for that nothing in particular
Anything returned there would be metaphoric hurt

2. invisible uniform

The piano was blind and heavy to lift
When imagining what colour was it played itself

Colour *itself* was in search of somewhere to settle
Passing as a logarithm over a field of touch-type clouds

3. invisible hell

Anonymous garden hassled into self-consciousness
Groans steadily with a potential for possession

Self-ridicule grows tired and babbles irrelevancies
Hydroponic deliberation propped against a lamppost

4. invisible example

Slack walls and relapsed corners
Those working in bed direct attention to distant peaks

Uninhabitable mirrors - predictable moons
Spoilt besmirched smudged unmade and fudged to fade

5. invisible context

If the signpost points to the suburbs
It probably does so without point or description

The pair currently resting are also currently at rest
Right-hand glove looks relaxed - the left one less so

6. invisible sun

Shop-front and shirt-front are not interchangeable
The too casual shopper turns into a slug

Forensic surrealism scours another *copse*
The postman as pale as a dawn a pig or a naked dog

7. invisible censorship

Leave me alone and let me dream
Even if it is of blood let me dream

Identity is a current of bum notes and mocktails
Sometimes leaking sideways into a pool for tadpoles

8. invisible analogy

Straight from the morgue to the jumble sale
A charming pair of boots all shiny and curled

Afternoon weaves a cobweb across the sun
All is autonomic deceit or Marxist charity?

9. invisible fashion

To be misunderstood is a privilege
Not available to most people during peacetime

Music from the radio fills the room with gold
Toothache raging but from no particular tooth

10. invisible seduction

The writer and the jetty exchanged stories
While the sea hummed laugher then howled it

Dripping joists and widowed struts of darkness
Splashed long shadows across the illegality of oaths

11. invisible life

Overwrought handiwork rotting in allotments
Cabbages flower in motionless midnight heaven

Waiting for us in our old cars - all our past dogs
We can only believe what nobody else could imagine

12. invisible night

The whimsy of apathetic madness
Becomes the excitation of unspoken riddles

Ghosts delayed in the corridors of the old hospital
Will finally be demolished by blaspheming builders

13. invisible palindrome

Suction – everything going smoothly then?
Machines made of coughed mud sputter copies

More devices blink wink clang click whir buzz or burr
Muttering back-to-back about preciousness and thorns

14. invisible ground

The polished song of fertility connives with realism
To be a baby blackbird trapped in the conservatory

Just because the singer burns out before the song
Doesn't mean you shouldn't follow her example

15. invisible laws

The shrewdness of making music and chutney
Fools aliens into thinking we're harmless

Sun going down hidden by this hill
Irradiating magnetic reptiles climbing tall towers

16. invisible beauty

Waiting for the firework display - trees fidget
Further into the forest memory is sleeping

A dream is all interior *like* a calf on a cattle trail
A novel minus its empty rooms and hitchhiking fish

17. invisible journey

Nothing in particular was still hanging around
Surrounded by bitching sticklers for detail

Gymnasts of fur and feather jump waterfall
Dancer dances a bit of both with a clean and decent dance

18. invisible paper

Horses crossed the river for luck not for fortune
If something is missing it's probably the planet

Mermaid diarrhoea fertilizes our fields
Go once around the course then sheer off on a tangent

19. invisible committee

An unpeopled audit orchestrates the thermals
Armour of loose shingle and brackish mine-water

Drink up – you have an obscure ambition
Mountain ridge unstitched with frostbitten fingers

20. invisible fusion

Prophesy coiling towards its own heat death
Elides the drunkenness of its original human voice

The deserts of Greenland and jungles of Mars
Swop cocktails in the bar of misshapen starlight

21. invisible constellation

We will now *open the floor* for questions
Yes, the man at the back there with the scrubbed lapels

Why does a kicked dog sleep at its master's feet?
Because *Sir* it's probably as dead as my guillotined tie

22. invisible film

Biased fountain during visionary pain control
Pimps the subconscious

The beach sneaks behind the seafront
To steam open a secret shared with ambushed jellyfish

23. invisible force

Failure to see pleasure's limits feels (it) in the dark
Sword swallower tried it with a rusty ski stick

The thrust and parry of children's argument
Scrambles a spitfire too heavy with glue to attempt take-off

24. invisible reflection

The crack of bamboo - the tread of guile and guilt
A burning stage in a flooded palace

Dancers' legs broken hopping across rock pools
For those who linger - sunset seen from a street corner

25. invisible politics

A simply dressed man clowning around
For no one in particular in a generic street

The man goes home to paint his face
In the mirror the stillness of his world suspends all fear

26. invisible distraction

The post office is split into 2 then 4 then 6 then 3
Flick-book days calculate the cheapness of bombs

Any horizon around the corner will be hopelessly far
Return to the record shop – renew your search there

27. invisible script

Shivers sift the feathers of this hounded art
Thousands of sad fucking forms glibly shape-shift

And no particular foreign city writes home to dissemble
And no singular gardener marries her man

28. invisible threat

The insulting little stream at the back of the house
Is lucky to be both talented and changeable

Enquiring how animals can think without language
Is only important when we are this happy

29. invisible diamond

The challenge to cut a sponge into a sharp point
Eventually drags all spaceships to their doldrums

Drowned clouds – Tidal light – Treetops
A referent in free-fall no longer capable of breaking rules

30. invisible dance

The relationship between seafront and the sea
Is a facsimile of that between tea cup and tea?

Blazing newsprint café - playscript left on a table
Moves to the chair then to the door then to the wind

31. invisible value

Pegged and gleaming forth fourth in the row
Subdivisions board Am-Dram coach to the sports field

Petrol to keep the funfair returning here forever
Not yet found for anything newer than is necessary

32. invisible philosophy

The tower *grinds* to a halt for no particular reason
It could just as well have stopped without grinding

It could just as well have waited here for a reason
The tower is like a train – The train is like a tower

33. invisible nature

Sunbathing misery within imperfect science fiction
High on the cliff behind you - a perfect kitchen sink

Inaudible disapproval - worst enemy's deaf lightshow
Regional Anglo-after-hours *Nouveau Roman*

34. invisible clone

Auras – chain ferry – haunted engines
The links relay the murmurs beneath the mumbling

Other loops suggest the printing of postage stamps
Chessboards are for swimmers detained for questioning

35. invisible masthead

Dry gradations slot into *watery graves*
Longship slips into rivermouth (last year its hips stuck)

This butterfly search for a suitable size
Comes to rest on a flower already buckling beneath beauty

36. invisible blood

Wallowing in self
Acidic cold flash circles to collide with its own spores

The Dog Whistle of Spades runs with the hyena's Heart
The Dingo of Diamonds runs with the jackal's Club

37. invisible home

Vertically spectral on a twilight canal bank
Neither floating nor standing nor alone nor attached

The snooker game made the pint last a long time
Some things are only ridiculous when repeated

38. invisible group

Sunday afternoon in sunny long-ago spring
Chuck Berry's *No Particular Place to Go*

No one had a car but we could imagine the seat-belt
Walking radio weightless - fiddling with transistor

39. invisible totem

Poems made from a past want a stake in the future
The room as crowded and stuffy as an owl's nest

Lovers on the beach witness the birth of philosophy
Lovers on the beach witness the death of philosophy

40. invisible permission

Clouds shout – silkworm journalists boil
A creeping Jesus congeals into the hack's verses

Aliens in class photo shake tails and rustle filaments
Snakeskin time capsule processed and popped

41. invisible poverty

Caress of the rhino plus escaping carcass gas
Taxi picks-up and drops-off a hollow wisdom tooth

Fulsome film made with wispy adverts wins prize
Déshabillé fuel running low – take cover inside the bladder

42. invisible flag

The Theatre of Curiosity – pretend you're a scorpion
Simplifications may mislead in poetry as well as in science

Scrap of used notepaper blowing about on the beach
Blows inland and out of reach

43. invisible mirror

Motorcycle's dream has to search through its history
Though its wheels only take it so far

What the wise man says gets shorter and shorter
Traveling east towards the reverb of western canons

44. invisible river

Hostilities from locals loyal to a long-dead god
Forced us to find a new way to fund our hospitals

Geese and geysers made of gold are not golden
A discovery immediately gone but never forgotten

45. invisible heaven

Remember blades of grass in the washing-up bowl
Sunset burning a tramp's hair as he pushed his bike

Is retrospective love really possible?
Ask the signature tunes of ice-cream van and fire engine

46. invisible star

The yard is roughly twelve metres by seventeen
Does that make you picture a yard that's a bit rough?

Does it make you think something else entirely?
A possibility of measuring language always somewhere nearby

47. invisible anarchy

He hasn't touched his beer but he will
He briefly touched his salad unconsciously

In this world there is belief in chips burgers and service
This man manages to talk of many things at once

48. invisible evidence

Trays of chocolate cigarettes left out in the rain
A big hotel on the seafront blocks out the sun

This pub is on Station Rd. and is near the station
If I already knew its name the pub would be a two-faced liar

49. invisible translation

Orchards of holes cut from daguerreotype tramlines
Thieves are operating in this area

Wassailing as perfectly as is humanly possible
While under a drug simulating deja vu and petrichor

50. invisible mirage

The ocean that brings in the town's clouds
Deposits runaway's pawnshop on the airport runway

Fuck off boss go screw your *apolitical* self
Haggard asteroids flare into life - existential splendour

51. invisible shrine

The light and the dark tremble with uncertainty
Good and evil marking each other's exam papers

Focus any border's fuzz into the rarest refinement
A hungry wolf is the harshest of the brotherhood of judges

52. invisible fruit

Circus Police impound hot hotdog van
Hell full of stuff the prophet never meant to say but did

Where in hell is hell if not in what we paid to watch?
Crowd coming out of cinema - the light still too strong for stars

53. invisible skin

Cumbersome badger clique empty for everyone
Office Supplies is a store of brittle transparencies

Organs into dust – function into freedom
The head is drunk but rides on the body of an athlete

54. invisible geometry

Stilted hugs and squishy triggers
Stalactites in attic should now be as soft as old carrots

The hilt of this sword is made of goosebumps
Baked hard at noon on a bed of low tide grass blades

55. invisible crime

Shrill even when transferred to paper
Sanctimonious designs of the Company Director

Voiceover falters over information left in latrines
Professionalism failing badly in a 24-hour lucid dream

56. invisible information

Let's eat the winners of the literary prizes
It may limit conversation but we can take some snaps

Here's a *particularly nice one* of *Seasons at Sea*
Coffee maker abandoned beside a bicycle behind a barn

57. invisible list

Arid Martian delta sunk half-way to the sea
Eden for masochists turns up our *not that interested* noses

At least one old night smuggled in by one new day
The *stroll in the trees* comes out in *The Unknown University*

58. invisible embroidery

A giggle of children trickles down the back lane
Is this an urban or a rural back lane?

A million demonstrators vanish into backstreet maze
Clapperboard – CCTV – Sandwich board – Torture

59. invisible enemy

Clocks don't tick they twitch then stutter
Dismantle the barricade then re-erect it further back

Clocktower shadow cuts across sundial
Fill-in the graves with our fresh revolutionary gossip

60. invisible victory

Reality soaked in the fantasy blood of profit
Scratches the surface of an identical universe

All those exterminated romantics reappear
Masturbated into being by the lifeguard's jazz-hands

61. invisible death

Just 'cause you're scathing about the Roller Coaster
Doesn't give you the right to deny Jesus Christ

Oh yes it does it does it does yes it does oh yes it does
It is that very thing that gives me that very right

62. invisible window

Greenfinch scrawls a detour around a flaw in the flow
Sifts apparent silence - the terrifying vibration of deceit

Crawl back to the hotel with other tired tourists
Lift your eyes to the empty glass cabinets in the foyer

63. invisible critique

I crave being brave and adventurous again
Nobody pays attention when the air is this fearless

Once I plucked well weathered words from *a* Pacific
Picked specifics to pieces with my diamond plectrum

64. invisible shade

Chip-fryer fat blob and splatter - parasitic visions
Brain parade in paradise - body burns on beach

Tepee pyre erected on the yacht's decking
Cerebellum's lungs topped-up from steaming ocean

65. invisible problem

If you insist on putting one word in front of another
At least try to resist their significance

Folded-up dummy in chestnut brown suitcase
One word behind another enough to put you in your place

66. invisible duplicate

Galley rowed by enslaved caterpillars takes flight
Just as suddenly as this surprise was expected

But in the rusty grout and drizzle of a hotel parking lot
Granular figments drive time through water boatman rain

67. invisible road

Days of vacuum – the mystery of concentration
Habits of the sky form a dense pile in the corner

On the day I die the universe's future *can* commence
On the day you die the universe's future *will* commence

68. invisible fate

The wit of the parasite is some compensation
The painted pebbles are those glazed with water

Peripatetic slander lands on its final victim for the day
Pretty stone thrown back into wave dropped into pocket

69. invisible terror

Late to the party plate tectonics
Litter left on beach - early morning crop of stubble

Stickmen strip poker – insects investigate
Ingrowing toenail levered free by the Ace of Spades

70. invisible pride

The half-volley triumphant
A dune filtered through a description of eyelashes

Twilight still sleeps - sunburnt
Night falls through the foliage with a modest cry

71. invisible pool

Fish have faces more human than some humans
Some humans' faces resemble hung wet rags

From the escalator's empathy to the futile date
The 18th stranger of the day emerges from a grey swamp

72. invisible paradox

A phrase compacted into a single word
Explodes with more explanations than necessary

The blind lecturer knows exactly what he's saying
Though no particular student is more or less listening

73. invisible clarity

Even pavement leads to cobbled quayside
Stomach juices undulate and slop against loops

What I mean is even the pavement leads there
Galloping towards retirement home – horse eclipses horse

74. invisible junction

What this street needs: a canal with supernatural wind
A squall of liquid liberty sculpted into ice blocks

Baskets of coal buckets of seaweed
Unearthly crust forming on the hours they have left us

75. invisible smile

The old road into the mountains is coming soon
A ceremony of hilltop bathing for the suffering

Emotion on hold helps argument kick ladder away
Mentally I'm as healthy as a row of colour-coded rubbish bins

76. invisible duet

Every column is a chimney - hot anger released
Today the sea is too bright to look at

X-rayed man with a spine of smoke signals
Trades an anchor thrust in pebbles for a beach of potatoes

77. invisible title

Impatient filming of the building site theatre
If the uniqueness of each dust particle is up for debate

Anonymous ideas maintain the equilibrium
This particular photo decorated with dictating droplets

78. invisible conformity

Brain made of glass in a head made of shadows
Stone pounding patterns on drumskin of analytic slippage

Medals hungover from last night's poem
Help the managers of authenticity refurbish their protocols

79. invisible revolution

Heart-breaking honesty of Monday's detritus
Registers in Tuesday's symptoms as great ape regicide

Wait long enough and the week will finish early
Without a latest grief for the electrons in your flesh

80. invisible space

Inner organs of marble and bronze
Encased by wood pulp and triangular parrot juice

Whatever you were thinking is s e v e r e d
Understudies and subs – innocent, watchful, squared

81. invisible invitation

Limpet kiss chain – drowned valley drowned gods
Avalanche of ultramarine nick-knacks

A massacre of innocent earthenware
A wet wool miniskirt saying Mass over a rockpool

82. invisible mountain

Little lung takes a bath with the whales
Title for the new grouping is *An Impression of Standards*

Debris settles – Thought settles
Settee left on the tip sings *it's always spring out here*

83. invisible prize

You have to put yourself out there
Among the seagulls and flattery of crashed planes

Landfill perfumes articulate planetary appetites
A word shared by different languages is an agitation

84. invisible melancholy

Our terror was humiliated
It osculates its origins with our position in the queue

Grills that question what cell type they block
Inundated with gold bars pearls and argent truffles

85. invisible game

I'm only androgynous when swimming
Elation starts all over again with the parting of the...

There was a fire damaged box camera and chess set
And a pale green demob case still strapped and buckled

86. invisible sky

Slow relaxed rain falling on engraved anagram
An escape to the tower – a high and airless window

Whatever picture that picture brings to mind
It will never replace the magic biography's street brawl

87. invisible currency

Ratings croon the ship rat's lullaby
Facetious workshop remark leaves no jaw beneath beard

Snails glue themselves to the goodwill of the cross
The crew coming ashore - pelicans jostle their corsets

88. invisible map

Pocket-size version of immense smoking vestige
Scratched binocular lens metres within millimetres

The *verge of tears* edits diameters off a shoal of giants
The book is an accretion - a well-greased *body of work*

89. invisible mask

A natural saucepan and an unnatural boat
Joke about what they could have for dinner tonight

As a slapdash campsite the sea is an abstraction
The cliffs in darkness now a sculpture garden of dangers

90. invisible flood

I think humidity thinks it's not unfriendly
Episodic necessity – orchestra shrinks or swells

Rocks muster around a cluster of impressions
Sirens buzz in and out of the hole in the guitarist's head

91. invisible prison

Bopping side-saddle on perpetual motion fluting
Partial view from here a consequence of resentful voting

Who or what does the black flag represent today?
Psychological test weeds out public poets from part-timers

92. invisible flower

A private chemistry behind a featureless heap
Funnels lethargic echoes through desire's reflections

Low tide – mirage – egg-timer clogging
At least those boys deprived of love have been let down gently

93. invisible failure

Washed up on the steps as tidal as emigration
The stairwell not always such an underused suntrap

Washed out poems as wished away as written was
Fireman – Barber – Lighthouse Keeper – Pole-vaulter

94. invisible index

Council house starlings circle the estate
Children time their arrival in the street to match mine

Only those who walk see the little sidewalk landscapes
We don't say sidewalk here we say sleeping typesetter

95. invisible darkness

Sunset skipped from bay to bay
Beneath the scalp sunrise sides slides shifts and sprays

Gravity - high-viz jacket - conspiracy
The over-experienced yet underused home-phone

96. invisible exhibition

Sand dribbles across the cosmos
From bypass roadkill to the Natural Futurology Museum

Hobby jockey jumps over eventuality blister
Hobbyhorse laughing through its teeth at their private joke

97. invisible image

Regaled by beggars in time-lapse profile
Badminton pigeons alarmed by the size of the knots

Pigeons play underarm beach-volleyball in the street
No particular street and no particular pigeon

NOTES:

Poem 23 invisible force – Incident in childhood while playing sword fighting with an actual 'rusty ski stick'. Somehow I managed to strike my opponent at the back of his mouth. He went to hospital and I was in Big Trouble.

Poem 27 invisible script – the 'hounded art' is poetry.

Poem 34 invisible clone – The 'chain ferry' is the Torpoint Ferry between Cornwall and Devonport that I travelled on daily for 9 years.

Poem 57 invisible list – In The Stranglers version of 'Walk On By' before Dave Greenfield's extended organ solo Hugh Cornwall snarls that he is going to *take a stroll in the trees*. 'The Unknown University' is the title of what is essentially Roberto Bolano's collected poems.

Poem 82 invisible mountain – appeared on my fb page.

Poem 85 invisible game – The 'fire damaged box camera and chess set' were salvaged by my Grandad from a air-raid fire in Portland dockyard. He was supposed to be the warden but the story is he stayed fast asleep while the bombs fell. The 'pale green demob case' was my Dad's. He had been in the Navy.

Poem 89 invisible mask – This was written in response to some lines by Luke Emmet.

www.ingramcontent.com/pod-product-compliance
Lightning Source LLC
Chambersburg PA
CBHW042337040426
42446CB00021B/3480